JYOTIMA FLAK

THE MINI-COURSE METHOD

HOW YOU CAN BUILD UP A 5/6 FIGURE
ONLINE BUSINESS WITH PRODUCTS
FOR UNDER 30 DOLLARS

Design: JyotiMa Flak, Fotos: Gaby Schütze
Translation into English: Stephanie A. White

ISBN: 978-3-9821560-5-7

Photo: Gaby Schütze

BE A LIGHTHOUSE, NOT A TEA LIGHT!

BEST WISHES, JYOTIMA

CONTENTS

CONTENTS:

INTRODUCTION

You have a unique gift that wants to be made visible to the world!
What's the point if you want to keep your unique gift for just a small
handful of people?

Show yourself! and let lots of people share your valuable knowledge.
Just imagine selling your courses on a daily basis - with social media,
this is possible! Because you can earn money with every link that you
build into your social media profile - try it!

Maybe you normally have a coaching program and you want to
expand your business - Maybe you are right at the beginning and
don't understand where you should start or what with…

As a business mentor I can tell you: Develop high-end products and
begin on a 1-1 basis.

As an entrepreneur and with the experience of the last 2 years my advice
is - to create Mini-Courses, let thousands of customers find you, and then
earn money every day!

With a sales funnel that works for you on a daily basis.
The Mini-Course Method!

You will learn how that works and how you can produce a Mini-Course in
24 hours and then immediately earn money online (possibly 5-6 figures in
addition to your normal products) in this book.

Yours, JyotiMa

18
19
20
21

1. WHY YOU DON'T NEED FREEBIES ANYMORE

When I started my online business in 2011 it was all about creating leads! (Email addresses).

I spent days working on creative ideas with my mastermind colleagues, creating marketing funnels based on the freebie - the free gift for the email address - hello client! It took 5-8 months in my newsletter before a client bought anything from me, sometimes even longer.

Since the GDPR was introduced, this marketing instrument has died. The freebie is no longer allowed to be linked to the newsletter and has made it more complicated to simply exchange an email address for a freebie. Of course, there are still freebies that work really well and I use these as well.

However, in this book, I want to show you a new way. A method that bypasses the undecided and attracts the client that wants to buy into your sales funnel. Clients that will give positive feedback once they have received your course and will gladly buy further products from you.

I call them Superfans and this book is all about how to find these clients and how to build up a 5-6 figure business.

2. THE MINI-COURSE METHOD

I have been working with Mini-Courses since 2019. My first course came onto the market right on time for the start of the Corona Pandemic in March 2020!

I found it easy to introduce several small products onto the market regarding online business and social media. With the result that I had 34% more turnover in 2020 and I even doubled that in 2021.

I had to cancel all of my live events because of Corona so instead, I sold small online courses. I sold on Sundays whilst going for a walk, and my daughter was ecstatic when I bought her an extra big ice cream to celebrate. „Catching", is the sound that your mobile makes when your payment provider informs you of a sale.

I'm talking about Mini-Courses! Small online products that you want to buy directly you see the advert - without thinking about it a great deal.

Products worth between 5-50 $, maybe even up to 70 $. The so-called „No-Brainer-Product" - is called that because you don't think about whether you really need it. It is so appealing and so full of content, that you buy it like „it's going out of fashion".

The mini offer can be: an E-Book, a Mini-Course, an Audio-Course, prepared texts, a Workbook, a Mini-Workshop, a paid challenge, text ideas for Social media, a photo filter, a content calendar, and much much more I'm sure that you have bought a product like this in the last time?

3. FUN AND TURNOVER WITH MINI-COURSES

Punctually at the start of the Corona pandemic, I had just organised a fully automated Member area. In just a few months, several hundred people had followed my mini products into this member area.

• First with **365 Content Ideas for Social Media**, ready-made ideas for social media (E-Book plus extras) that can be used for a whole year. Price: 27 $ net.

• I made my first upsell with an appealing 5 $ E-Book: **7 Lighthouse-Tips** for becoming more visible.

• Then I launched the **TikTok for Online Business** course. (one of the first TikTok courses in the german speaking area). Price: 57 $ net. As an Upsell, there was the above-mentioned product.

• A few months later **the Superfan funnel** came out, a course, in which I explain in more detail how funnel marketing works for your true target audience of Superfans. As an Upsell, the two Mini-Products above were used.

The result at the end of the year:

• 25 % of clients bought three to four Mini-Products.
• 55 % of clients bought two Mini-Products.
• Some even bought all of them or came into further groups.

• Some booked the 1-1 Online Business-Mentoring-Programme for 3-6 Months = **dream clients!**

To a large extent, my Mini-Course clients are enthusiastic followers that comment on articles and that recommend my courses as affiliates.

Customer love!

I really enjoyed this time. I could inspire even more people. I also have the impression that I have enough aces up my sleeve to take my business to the next level. The courses work passively in the background preparing the ground for my dream client.

Through my visibility on Social Media, the Mini-Courses are always present, even without a launch or that I do active advertising.

I continue to sell courses on Sundays while I go for walks with my daughter … fully automatically. **Understand?**

4. WHAT IS A SALES FUNNEL?

A sales funnel collects your target group and ideally converts them into your client.

Everything that interests your client about your subject goes in the top. You attract your target audience with exciting content and tips (posts, blogs, videos, podcasts, or adverts). The more they see of you the more they interact with you and build up confidence.

That's the rough outline anyway.

Until someone decides to buy there are usually at least 7 forms of contact - therefore 7 types of visibility of you. Then your followers sign up for a freebie from you. So you still haven't totally gained their confidence.

5-8 months passed until just before the Mini-Course a potential client was willing to sign up for a free consultation. This client had been following all my steps and watched until the right offer appeared before taking action.

By getting to know your target audience, and how they communicate and react, you can accelerate this process. And the quicker you have your Superfans!

Look at how urgently your followers are looking for solutions, and move through your funnel. How quickly they are ready to buy Mini-Products and high-priced coaching?

Distance yourself from the competition and show your values and what makes you - you! Attract YOUR Superfans!

I have shortened the 'customer journey' (the journey the client goes through until he buys from you) from five to eight months down to zero to two months!

Visitors to my website immediately buy a low-priced Mini-Product - because they are curious. Often the next sale takes place within two months.

Many of the Mini-Course clients are interested in other mentoring or group programs. They are ready to grow.

Trust is already there through the Mini-Product (the first solution achieved!) and the willingness to take a bigger step with you is there.
Begin with a first small Mini-Product on your social media profile. Your funnel also begins here. The link is the key.

An automated funnel - yes or no?

Build the funnel for your followers to be as automatic as possible without becoming a machine. Stay available, stay close.

Timed actions and challenges attract your tribe and build up your community. This way you can react to changes and be active for the fans, for example in a Facebook group.

Renew the automated funnel on your website once a year and continue to expand it.

Paid advertising can be a tool to continually bring new clients into your funnel. Or you go the content strategy way with inspiring content, podcasts, blogs, and videos that get more and more of a range. Keywords, hashtags, SEO, and tags in videos help to bring your target audience to you.

I recommend paid adverts AND organic traffic the more followers you get the better.

For the Mini-Course funnel, **you need to pay for advertising,** this is a part of the funnel.

AD

5. THE 1. SALES FUNNEL, REIMBURSES YOUR ADVERTISING BUDGET

The aim of your Mini-Course funnel is to bring back your Ad-Budget!
What, only the Ad-Budget? - Yes, in the first instance.

Have a little patience. Everyone that buys a Mini-Product has the potential of becoming a Superfan. Every third or fourth client will probably buy three courses. But for that, you need the second step.
Now you need to take the plunge.

Maybe you already know that feeling from buying shares or
crypto-currency. ;-)

You put everything on one card. Invest a minimum of 500 $ in advertising. Even better would be to do this several times consecutively per Mini-Course. You set up an advertising campaign for your first Mini-Product which has the most potential.

If you have no idea how to do this then it's best to hire an advertising specialist (for example by the hour).

In my case, I used an 11-$ E-Book as a tool. I invested 500 $ and wanted to sell as many E-Books as possible (at least 46 books but of course preferably more) The idea was to sell as many as possible. To gain E-Book-clients and to fill my email list with excited Superfans.

Write four different texts and create several different motives. Also, make several videos, videos always run better than adverts.

You can also create some story ads. Canva gives you several really good ideas you can use. You will find the link to Canva at the end of this book under tools.

When you do videos make sure you add subtitles. I add the subtitles on my smartphone with the Apps: Captions, CapCut, or Inshot (Like TikTok videos).

You can also upload videos to Facebook and add the subtitles there and then advertise via the advertising manager (don't go via the button advertise this post you can lose a lot of money like this).

Remember to renew your adverts after 7 days. Create further motives and add the same call to action: Buy a Mini-Product, learn more!

Another tip: limit the offer to 7-9 days. You can trigger a buy impulse like this - Only available until XXXX get yours now!

Tell your story behind the product and make the product tangible.

The first sentence in the text should be the 'hook'. This is how you get your followers to read the advert and get their attention.

Example:
• Stop! don't continue reading if…..
• It sounds so ridiculous: This method generated 35% more turnover for me.
• Wow, I never lost weight this fast before!
• What she experienced then, changed her life!
• Do you want to achieve XYZ? I'll show you how here.

Which of these phrases did you react to? make a note of them so you can find your ideal strategy. It's possible that your client will find the same things interesting as you - isn't it?

The adverts are an Investment in the growth of your business. Believe it. Always imagine that every advert increases the chances of wonderful results with your target group.

Your future clients wouldn't have found you without your adverts. You are becoming visible.

And then we have the upsell. Plan to offer further courses as soon as this campaign has run. Low-cost, high-quality useful courses, provided your target group is willing to invest in their further education!

I personally put the focus on quality, design and content. I could sell all my courses at three times price.

But I have a goal: **Happy Superfans!**

Let that be your goal too and offer even more proof of trust on your landing page.

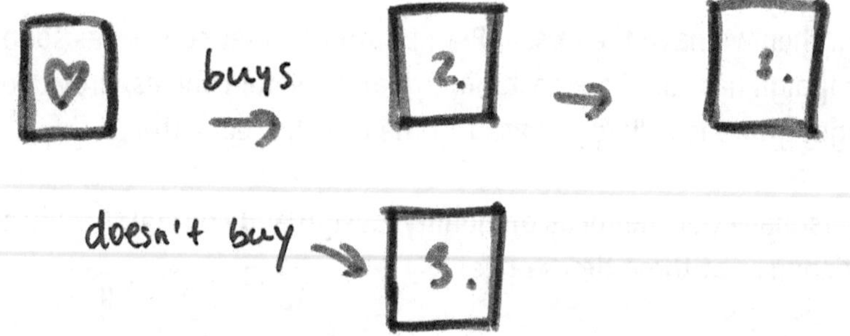

buys
2.
1.
doesn't buy
3.

6. THE UPSELL

The most important thing is that you use an automated payment provider. You can add additional automated sales funnel tools later.

I created my funnel with Digistore24.com. A payment provider that I also use for my affiliate partners so that they receive a commission for advertising my courses. You can also use Stripe, Paypal, etc.

Every payment provider allows you to add upsells to your sales page.

Adding upsells.

The sales process:

Client buys Mini-Product – a./b.
a. 1. Upsell – buys – 2. Upsell, purchase confirmation
b. Doesn't buy – Down-sell, purchase confirmation

If a client buys this book via my landing page he is led to an upsell with a reduced follow-on course: **Your Mini-Course in 24 hours,** for 47,- instead of 149,-$ net.

If he doesn't buy, he receives a down-sell: **The 365 Content Ideas for Social Media,** for 19.90 instead of 27,-$ net.

If he also buys the **Mini-Course in 24 hours** he will receive a further offer: **Your Superfan-funnel,** a course that fits exactly to this book and exactly fills the gap to get more ideas for your offers. Price 47,- instead of 57,-$ net.

If he doesn't buy, the sales process ends and he is led to the thank you page and to the download of the E-Book.

I personally wouldn't do more than 2 upsells but try it for yourself and have several online courses ready on the sideline.

I recommend products costing a maximum of 250,-$. You can also offer a member area, a paid Facebook group, etc as an upsell. Further products which give more knowledge in your area. For this choose subjects that supplement, but don't overlap:

Mini-Course: E-Book / Tool-Kit with everything I need to know
Upsell 1: Practical course to deepen knowledge
Upsell 2: Member area to ask questions and for support, or a further learning course with a slightly different focus.
Downsell: Meditation, how to achieve your goal
For the upsell, you need a further 1-3 courses or products worth up to 250,-$.

Your Upsell-Ideas:

Your Upsell-Ideas:

7. THE 2. SALES FUNNEL, ATTRACTING SUPERFANS

There is another funnel that you should have. The client email list is really important and can be built up like this.

This is why the sales process should automatically be connected to your email provider. All clients will automatically be included in your newsletter list.

Tip: You do this with the API (Application programming interface) connection from the payment provider to the Newsletter. Produce a list of clients, preferably per course so that you have a better overview.

You can now start offering upsells during a sales process. You can also add an upsell, days, weeks, or even months later depending on how quickly you have completed the courses.

Tip: You shouldn't leave too much time between adding the upsells. I recommend no more than four months, don't forget you want to sell more than one course. Work on several courses at the same time and build your funnel like this from the beginning.

Develop an unerring strategy to attract your clients, and your future Mini-Course funnel plan, see chapter 14.

Offer a further product (next price sector 70-297,- $).
You can of course sell products up to approximately 2000,-$.

After every step invite to a webinar or a free consultation. Ask your clients if they are willing to work with you.

You could also work with the email route after the first Mini-Product. For this, write at least 5 emails. Tell your story, and allow the client the chance to really get to know you. lead them to a further solution in their development with your subject You can of course sell courses one at a time, your email list is full of people that will be happy to remember you.

From my experience, it works best if the prices aren't too far apart and too high. You don't want to scare off your Superfans.

Allow your Super-fans time, let them think about whether they are willing to recommend you or to buy your higher-priced product. For the small prices, you will find a mass of buyers that can become great multipliers.

Get course!
Buy now!
click!

The strategy for your Mini-Course sales funnel:

Extra

8. BONUS BONUS BONUS

Isn't it great when someone prepares something special for you?
Why don't you add a bonus call? A workshop or a webinar? This can also
be prepared in advance (you lead onto a page where the workshop can
be watched.

You do this directly after the product has been bought or a couple of days
later (don't miss your bonus!) e.g.

A 30-60 minute video of you in which you explain your methods in detail.
In this, you can also talk about your higher-priced product.
Or you add a free consultation regarding the course, to discuss `if they-
want to achieve further goals with you.

Tip: In these situations, you can sell your higher-priced content.
You can also send vouchers for your next course or event.

Of course, the webinar can be live. I am trying to allow ideas to develop
how your funnel can work for you automatically while you eat home-
made strawberry tartlets :)

To create an automated webinar you only need a ready video on an appealing webpage that can be accessed via a link in for example an email.
You can also use webinar tools to filter visitors and where you have
functions like time limitations, webinar at a particular time, after signing
in, etc.

7 bonus ideas for your Mini-Course:

1.

2.

3.

4.

5.

6.

7.

9. THE RANGE OF COURSES FOR YOUR EXPERT STATUS

Make your clients happy with amazing content and sell them what they need for their journey. Take them with you on the journey.

Instead of a generalised course in which you find everything including the kitchen sink.. produce more specialised offers starting from very small to big!

This way your offers will be more focused. One product = one result! Then the next offer. You know the word niche. Stick to producing niche products, instead of trying to pack everything into one course.

For example, one product covers the subject of video production for social media, another the subject of video techniques, and yet another covers the mindset needed for the video appearance. As a follow up you can offer a mastermind course. And don't forget, the E-Book with the best video tools can be downloaded for 9,-$

You get expert status if you have a good range of products. Several books and other products.

Become an expert in your area. Show your knowledge in complete and ready courses!

Tip: I am often invited to co-ops by other experts, - online course bundles, online conferences, etc.

It's great if I can then offer my latest course with a price reduction or free of charge.

Online conference organisers are interested in experts with a ready-to-go product range so that they can receive a commission on the sales of the products.

On top of that, chances of becoming more visible and of getting an expert status. **The world is waiting for you!**

10. DEVELOPING AND COMPLETING COURSES IN 24 HOURS

Take a guess - how long do you think it took to write this book?
A total of 10 hours then another 2 hours for the landing page, to create
the finished product and the connection to the member area.
My assistant did the copy reading and voila! finished.

A Mini-Course doesn't have to be completely finished and etched into
stone- it's not the Sistine chapel, it's a Mini-Course! It can have just a
few sections to it.

But stick with what is written on the website, the more detail the better.
You want the product to be described in detail and that it's absolutely
clear that it will be delivered like that.

Think of your happy client. You want him to be ecstatic about the value
for money that he is getting. The goal is to over-deliver. Give your client
more than he was expecting.

I have digital courses falling out of the sky. I have lightening ideas (while
asleep;)) and then create them within one or two weeks, the longer the
course takes the more difficult it is usually to sell.

So, how do you get ideas for Mini-Products?

Make a list:

• What does your tribe need first, what would be the first step?
• What is a part of your overall program anyway and what can you build up to be for example a first module or an E-Book?
• Have you just held a workshop that you could easily transcribe?
• Do you already have an amazing meditation regarding money awareness?
• Can you take 5 of your blogs, posts, or videos and combine them to form a course?
• Now write down ten ideas on how you can do good for your target group or what you can offer in a few hours:

1.

2.

3.

4.

5.

6.

7.

8.

9.

10.

The Name:

What shall we call the baby? It doesn't have to be all that serious.
Fitting to the price it is allowed to be comical and fun. Have fun with
your creation. Think about it again, this is just the beginning, you can
produce a new course every 2 months, think about the shining eyes of
your Superfans when there is a cool new product to discover. Surprise
them with your ideas!

Now look for what you need in terms of technical tools
• Email provider
• payment provider
• Member area, possibly connected to a payment provider
• Content like E-Book, videos, audios, pdfs
• BONUSES
• Landing page
• Adverts
• Emails
• Social Media
There is more information regarding technical tools at the end of
the book.

Name and content of your product:

11. HOW DO YOU CREATE A MINI-COURSE?

Have you collected the contents and put them together? Did you find one or two ideas in the ten you wrote down that immediately sounded cool and fun?

Exercise: is there energy on it? Close your eyes and breath, then, when you open them again which three courses do you immediately look at, that almost seem to glow before your eyes? Make a circle around those courses. Which one you you want to start with? Which one could be an upsell? Mini-Book upsell for 5$ or a further course or meditation on top? Ready to Rumble. Now put your course together.

Be willing to combine different types of content: audio, video, pdf, look for pictures so that it is put together in an appealing way, or place value on the text and make sure it is professionally proofread.

Create an appealing design with Canva or Word and include pictures. More to this is in the technical tools section at the end of the book. Now you put everything together in a file or on the page of your membership area, your google drive or your password-protected website (this is also possible at the beginning).

After a sale, the client is led to this site or he is taken via the payment

provider's download - sale complete!
Now you start preparing the sales page and the sales campaign.
Start posting that something amazing will happen next week, begin
with the **launch!**

12. YOUR E-BOOK IN 48 HOURS

I have already said that you don't need to write a novel when writing an E-Book, 20-80 pages are totally OK.

You can then publish it via Amazon. Structure the contents.
What do the people want to know and what do they need to know?
Keep it short and to the point.

1. Formulate your synopsis, then work your way through it - Start, and have fun writing!
2. Collect your blogs and posts and recycle them.
3. Record it as audio and transcribe it.
4. Simply transcribe several of your videos or stories. You can recycle everything! It's your content!

I published a book bestseller full of 5-minute videos from the 20 experts that were part of my online conference. Everyone transcribed and of course, edited their contribution, and an Amazon paperback and E-Book with 208 pages was finished! which by the way became a bestseller! Amongst the contributors was the well-known author Dr. Rüdiger Dahlke.

I personally did not work on my contribution for more than 1,5 hours. Reduce your work to the minimum, have fun and get the most out of it.

You could write the following E-Books (collection of ideas):

1.

2.

3.

4.

5.

6.

7.

13. BONUS CHAPTER:- YOUR FIRST ONLINE COURSE IN 3 DAYS

You have started really well. The whole thing also works as an online course.

What does your target group need? Now develop an online course worth between 70- 297,-$.

Keep everything just as short as before and try to think of something low-cost which will generate cash flow. Think of your funnel that has to be completed!

The structure:

Which units does the course include? Does it have a duration? 7 days or 4 weeks? Organise the contents into units. Post-its help find a structure or just push notes back and forth on the floor.

The framework: record an intro in which you invite your client to take part in the course. At the end ask for feedback and pitch your free consultation (the next steps with you!)

Audio courses are more timeless than videos. You can record audio directly with your smartphone or with an external microphone.

Tip: Crawl under a blanket to record your audios, it's your own little recording studio.

Is there a pdf? Add your Logo and your Corporate design. Leave space for practice and thoughts and results that participants can write down.

Videos: Light, light, light!

Is your room light enough? Otherwise, put up softbox lights and pay attention to the sweat on your face.
Create a calm environment, neither too empty nor too busy:
No-gos: shelves, over full rooms, not enough light, cheap furniture
Don`t give the viewer any chance to be distracted or think about the environment. It should be high quality and neutral.

Welcome: a plant in the background creates a scale and is harmonious.
Your clothes: no small patterns, look at the clothes in the video and decide on your branding colours or accessories in the fitting colour.
Girls: Use light reflecting makeup foundation for smooth blemish-free skin (also possible for men). Lipstick and rouge can give your face contours.

It is important to use a microphone that is aligned to your voice.
Do a couple of tests before you record for hours.

Cut the videos at the beginning and end so that you have a clean start and finish. You can store your film on Vimeo as hidden or on Youtube as unlisted, then embed them in the Member area of your course.

A tip from 11 years of experience in online business: If something doesn't work, it is not a sign from the universe to give up!

OK!

That is in my course and this is how I am going to do it:

AD

14. YOUR MINI-COURSE SALES FUNNEL PLAN

Write down your future courses here and build up your Mini-Course sales funnel:

My first Mini-Product:

1. Upsell:

2. Upsell:

Smaller Product as a down-sell:

This is what happens after the sale:

Automatically: Emails automated bonus/workshop, Facebook group, etc.
This is what I will offer after the sale (e.g. 2 months later):

This is what I offer as a special offer once a year:

This is where the client finds regular content from me (Podcast, Youtube, Blog, Social-Media):

This is where I place the advertising for Mini-Product 1:
Which social media platform have you already posted on 100 times? have you looked after your profile regularly?

15. YOUR FEEDBACK

I will gladly post your feedback on this book on my website free of charge which equals: advertising for you on my website!

Answer the following questions:

1. This is how you felt before reading the book:

2. This is how this book has helped you (concrete example):

3. This is why you can recommend this book:

4. Your photo, name, description and website:
Please mail to: info@jyotimaflak.com

EPILOGUE

With this book, you really have the possibility to build up a 5/6 figure income or more within a couple of months.

And once you have set it up once, you know how a funnel works.
A successful online business begins with you and your power to implement. You now have the choice:

Alternative A:
You can immediately forget about this E-book and there still won't be any courses from you in the future

Alternative B:

You start getting and writing down ideas for Mini-Courses that you get under the shower, on waking up, or like me during a nap!

Hey, cool! Then start implementing this method immediately!

You can generate the first cash flow for your business like this and then scale up.

After a few weeks create the next course and keep doing this. Don't wait for the first one to become a huge success - just keep going and create one after the other.

With increasing turnover, you can make your funnel more and more

professional!
Go, Heart Business!

You can earn money on Sundays, or while you're asleep, the energy you
put into it will come back to you.
Building up an online business is always hard work, but the more
professional you become, (and the less perfect you want to be)
the more output you will achieve.

Which alternative are you choosing?

I would like to wish you the greatest success with the Mini-Course
Method! How did the sales funnel work for you? Write to me!
I would love to hear your feedback!

And if you want more: get yourself the follow-on course **Your Mini-
Course in 24h** or book a free conversation and let's do this together:
www.jyotimaflak.com

Light your online business on fire!

Be a lighthouse, not a tea light!

Your JyotiMa

JyotiMa Flak (Online Business Mentor & Author) she shows entrepreneurs how to attract clients and sell digital products online. Sign in to the newsletter so that you don't miss any upcoming offers anymore! www.jyotimaflak.com

You will find JyotiMa here:

www.jyotimaflak.com
www.facebook.com/jyotimaflakcom
www.instagram.com/jyotima.flak
www.pinterest.com/jyotima
www.youtube.com/jyotimaflak

www.tiktok-fuers-business.de
www.tiktok.com/@tiktoktipps_jyotimaflak

ADDITIONAL: TECHNICAL TOOLS FOR YOUR MINI-COURSE

Website:
Software: Wordpress.org
Theme DIVI www.jyotimaflak.com/divi

• Email provider:
ActiveCampaign, GetResponse, Aweber, MailChimp

• Payment provider (with upsell possibility):
Clickbank, Digistore24.com, Elopage

• Member area or covered by payment provider:
Kajabi, WishlistMember, Learndash, teachable

• Landing page:
LeadPages: www.jyotimaflak.com/leadpages
own Website with WordPress and theme DIVI www.jyotimaflak.com/divi

Funnel-Tools:
ClickFunnel

Sound:
• Mini-Microphone for Smartphone – Rhode Smart Lav:
https://amzn.to/2O0uQZt
• Podcast-Microphone – Audio-Technica AT2020 USB:
https://amzn.to/2QFJPJl

Lighting:
• Soft box lamp set: https://amzn.to/2KyHJry
• Ring light with tripod (at least 18 oder 20 inch):
https://amzn.to/31mwWu2
• Tripod for Smartphone or camera: https://amzn.to/343pqTd

Design tools:
• Canva – edit/design with pictures – www.jyotimaflak.com/canva
Desktop and Smartphone-App
• Pixaloop – convert photos into moving pictures
• Picsart – Storydesign

Videos:

Smartphone:
CapCut App – Cutting and editing Videos
Inshot – Cutting and editing Videos

Desktop:
Imovie – Mac-based cutting Programme for Films (free on Mac)
Vimeo Tools
Loom – Screen tutorials (free)
Zoom – Meetings and Webinars (Basic version free)

Notes:
• Evernote, filing für Notes, Desktop and Smartphone (free)
• Trello, filling Desktop und Smartphone, (free)

Some links are affiliate links, if you buy through this link I might receive a small commission.

Have fun with the tools and tag me when you have made your first Mini-Course or professional videos!

XOX, JyotiMa

www.ingramcontent.com/pod-product-compliance
Lightning Source LLC
LaVergne TN
LVHW011305210726
843509LV00016B/796